Love in the
Age of Unreason

Love in the
Age of Unreason

These are but wild and whirling words, my lord.

Shakespeare: Hamlet

Mike Johnson

Press

Published by 99% Press,

an imprint of Lasavia Publishing Ltd.

Auckland, New Zealand

www.lasaviapublishing.com

Copyright ©Mike Johnson, 2024

Cover Image: Leila Lees

ISBN: 978-1-991083-20-3

Street Corner Redoubt

Auckland – heritage hotel

1

I'm trying to fit myself
between the narrow spaces of the days
but I am fat from too many years
lounging in my think tank
trying to make amends
waiting for blessings to fall

>   even when I turn sideways
>   the hours squeeze me
>   in my indeterminate middle
>   where thought has grown sloppy
>   and age has taken its toll

I am trying to fit myself between
narrow wedges of buildings
but I'm too wide even for these parks,
boulevards, squares
and café riddled lanes

>   you couldn't swing a cat in this padded cell
>   or stuff your mind into the wardrobe

I am trying to fit myself into a life
someone else might have happily led
taking the carnivore for a walk on a leash

but can't face the heart-shape swirled onto the
surface
of a morning latte
the smell of stale sausage rolls
or the quivering sight of sad custard squares

> when I turn sideways, the mirror shames me
> while in the lift there is no sensation
> of movement
> just a sinking feeling in the gut

2

at night I dream of being lost
in strange cities, in the glaze
of eternal light
where even friendly strangers are no help

the more directions they give
the more confused I become

cluttered rooms lose me
in the cafés people put down their faces
and fondle their identity cards

busy streets hijack me
and intersections play noughts n' crosses
with pedestrians
it was not my choice to run these old gauntlets
of guilt and fear, fear and desire, desire
and death, death and love, church and state
reason and unreason

the dream didn't happen to me
I happened to the dream

3

In the wide-angle lens of the door's spyhole
there's a non-existent world
made only of hushed corridors, closed doors
and whispering carpets

while in the hubcap reflections of the street
the corners elude me - I can never see the world
in the round
with flat eyes

4

from a seat in Albert Park

I sit here where I've sat
many-a-time
watching the afternoon sun slip
between the mirror towers
contemplating the view
toward Vulcan Lane

I have a long history with myself here
watching and making up stories
I could tell when I got home
with the hopping of the blackbird and sparrow
a beer burning in my gut

on this seat, the past never dies
and the future never comes

a little rain
a woman's voice and heady scent
the rimu behind us having grown
just a few minutes older

we are just here then, you and I
nowhere else
prepared to let the rest rest
and take our chances
on ribbons of asphalt
memories of glass

fixless

sometimes there is, sometimes
there isn't
it's too busy playing hide and seek
among slabs of streets, compressed neon
people's words, and the wordless dance
of disasters in grayscale
extinctions in graphs

in that whole there are no nouns, or pronouns
just verbs in the continuous tense… seeing… feeling…
moving-being-having-losing
sounds that have no rest
on the homeless streets, the obdurate cement
the ghost-driven windows
and the empty bus stop
with its steel bench

there's no coming back to the subject
a kid with a slingshot has taken out the lights
the object has been scattered to the four directions
or totters home at the end of the night
with a luminous heart
clutched in two aching hands

there's no way of nailing anything down
that won't lift in the next storm

or be torn from your pretty fingers
as you lift the cherry tart to your lips

words find no rest, their relationship to the page
provisional and contingent, their relationship
to the air instant and dissolving
their relationship to memory
disputable

trying to make four dimensions out of two
we mistake the fixless for the fixed
the coming for the going
the having for the holding
nightmare's rainbow for pots of gold
glowing at the intersections

… the isn't for the is

stranded

there will never be another time
like this one
we will never arrive
at our starting point
and know ourselves for the first time
on streets we once saw as home
at the corner of Fort and Customs
where we ate chocolate cake
at a coffee shop
and talked of form and function
and the joys of creation

the hands of the clock by the Art Gallery
don't move in a circle
but spiral out of control
with the contrapuntal forces
of mind and memory
in and out of the cafés and convenience stores
malls and alleys
following ancient footsteps and
the clatter of bones

around the band rotunda, chairs rehearse their silence
a merry-go-round of faces fade like old leaves

we shuffle in and out of our lives
past Korean eateries and kebab houses

not knowing at which end to start
or how to make our way through a conversation
about love and children
lost opportunities, the tinsel hours
of Christmas

we won't reach the corner walking in this direction
methinks
where death seeps out of the tapa cloth
hanging in the gallery like a drying skin
and turning back won't help
for our footsteps have forgotten themselves
while Queen Street has vanished
into history's maze
and the murmur of commerce

the streets bend in the wrong direction
when you want to go the other way
buildings have assumed new identities
and traffic lights have reversed
their order of business

at the pedestrian crossing
children make a run for a new world
and something tasty
without a second thought

up the hill at Old Government House
history stands still in the musty order of business
and trees from other worlds stand guard
over the worn carpets of the Old Order

where beer was once served
to old scholars in Prufrock pants
and romance
came and went
between the first drink
and closing time

as we head across Albert Park
where lovers once lay between the shadows
heading for the wharf
like so many times before
I feel in my pockets for a couple of coins
to make an offering, an apology perhaps
to the Ferryman

burial ground

at every turn, hope hits a wall
neither this way, nor that way
nor the other way
no muddling through spaghetti junctions
throughways or viaducts
to come out the other side
carrying paper bags and hop cards

Shelly's fractured statue still gestures
to lone and level sands
although the shattered visage is now gone
the sneer of cold command
erased
message lost in new waves
of burning desert and more
blood

roads fry and buckle, the hammer melts
the last flood takes the bridge, the river runs red
the ferryman waits, dark holes for eyes
and points to the far shore
with a bony finger and an iron smile

talkers move their jaws
but their words are powdered glass
their breath stinks of methane
and bad dreams

children gather on the cusp, and stare
their faces smeared with ash
their bones on the outside of their bodies

the first and the last arrive at the same place
at the same time
their hands empty, their hands broken
their glaciers melted

like the emperors of old, our money ghouls
seek the secret of eternal life in perpetuation
of the flesh
for it rankles to know they can die
on their feather beds
just as easy as the homeless person
huddling on a mattress of cardboard

Balashikha

a boy and his mum woke up one morning
the house empty, the city empty
the sky empty, the gardens silent

the street and alleys, squares and parks
were sunk in powdery sunlight
in profound oblivion

when they tried to leave they found
that a mirror wall surrounded it
in an uncanny perfection of form

whatever they threw at the mirror
bounced right back at them
as if sprung from behind

they lived alone there for fifty years
and when the woman died, her son
abruptly
found himself back in the everyday world
of human sounds
but by then he was a man over sixty
and no one believed his story
despite a supportive DNA test

I often dream of that city
where I follow the wind down deserted streets
looking for directions
staring through windows at shadows
following the penumbra of the day
from light to dark

when I come to the mirror wall I stare at it
searching for an image

it's useless talking to things that can't talk back
I have to learn the language of silence
the nuances of shade
the eloquence of walls and doors
and unnerving intersections

over and over I tell myself
that my mother has died
and it is high time I
woke up

cross section

a grey limousine slides into view, windows darkened
the big wheel grinds to a halt
its seats rock the stars back and forth
life's hurdy-gurdy fading into space
above the mirror towers
nothing but floating debris

we are waiting for the music to begin again

nobody's come this way for quite some time
the dust is vintage
the silence matured in odours of decay
where the bodies are buried

trumpets and trombones, strike up the band!
here comes the ringmaster, dressed in black
the majorettes lift their skirts
the baton somersaults above a sky
painted in fading water colours

when the dead clap their hands
they make soft squishy sounds
melodies rise and fall from the old pianola

a man in orange cowboy boots steps out of the car
and onto the stage

the city breathes into the night
he gives the victory sign

sometimes the lies we let ourselves believe
are for our own good, we tell ourselves
the pauses are killing me
it's all about love in the age of unreason

lovers hold hands against time n' tide
their smiles are for eternity
a massive object bends light

it doesn't matter how many chairs you have,
you only have one arse, the beggar said
ghosts find a home behind windows

orphan words go crying down the street

the Holocene lies underneath the asphalt

the streets lie on the soft swell of hills
once made gentle by forests
and sweetened by spring winds
and brisk rains

(ah, yes, that's the kind of language we want
not lines of beggars dancing through the streets
tossing out skulls
a lolly scramble of fixed grins
while everybody toots their horns
in cacophonous rituals)

the streets lie on the soft breasts of hills
and down into once misty hollows
and the moist places where water was born

(ah yes, and love too, don't forget love words
slippery and strong, not lines that grind
over blacktop
in a city of concrete and ashes
and machine voices)

the streets trace the pathways of song
that lead the melody a merry chase
through pools of desire
and landscapes of feeling
the blessing of moving water
to the early world
and the first syllables
scratched on stone

the thief on Charm Street

a scroll-and-swipe doom loop culture
is their milieu
reset, reject, delete, swallow
and repeat

Impossible
Fairy Tales

Once upon a time

Dedicated to South Korean novelist Han Wujoo for
her novel *The Impossible Fairy Tale*

this way and that
over and above
there was and there was not
the wicked witch of the west
and the creatures she controls
the impossible fairy tale stretches credulity
seven with one blow!
twelve dancing princesses!
a hut that runs around on chicken legs
looking for children to eat

magpies peck at your banquet dreams
beloved
their sharp cries in black and white
Cinderella breaks her glass slipper
elves pack up their flowers
dwarves give away their gold

sleeping beauty climbs out of her grave
brought back to life by a kiss
and comes after you with an AK47
chattering a single syllable
over and over
nochildleftbehind, nochildleftbehind

moonlight shows the axeman
chopping at a tree that can't be felled
he grows weary with age
the axe heavy in his hand
the world heavy from grief
eternity is coming to an end
finally a reckoning
it may be god, rising from his coffin

bits of me play catchup
with the other bits
dust swirls up from the page
catch me if you can, I'm running bliss
I know a friendly fox who can take me
across the river on his snout
for free

from a tower window
the maiden lets down her hair
while the frog prince is erased by a kiss
love is here with the lords of misrule
in the age of disfluency
it's a default setting

stand this way and look the other way
the street takes a wrong turn
familiar things grow unfamiliar
in the semblance of the world
in the curve of the line
the curve of the road
where ordinary people stroll past

ordinary scenes
saying normal things to one another
in strolling voices
(you are not moving forward
things are moving backward)

foreground and background
change places and times
death is another way of breathing
an exhalation in your ear
the scene overflows
wherever your eye falls, clematis blooms
the greenfinch slipstreams, jewel of the wind
dragonflies hover over their shadows
nights collide
the homeless gather in doorways
a shapeless mass

in plain sunlight
the smell of jasmine grows stronger
tears cold and warm
warm and cold
(there is frost on the glass
frost scolds, tears swarm)

you believe by being not able to believe
accept
by being not able to accept
you fall out of your sentence
which comes into being as a way of seeing
you leave yourself behind

as you catch up with yourself
in flesh and thought
(I bend towards the music of shadows
dust on my fingers, fingers blind
and nails broken)

happy home happy life
eat together, stay together
gypsy girls swing their pony tails
children laugh and shout
and finish their battle in a tangle of knees
quick as a flick blackbirds appear at the open window
to peck at the soap

we won't reach the end beyond
the end
that is the impossible fairy tale
we seek to cover up or disclose
before our loves vapourize
and we run aground
(the particles of the scene are sinking
innumerable snowflakes blossom)

stand that way and look the other way
at right angles to the eye
I am erased as a pronoun
as a proper noun
but turn pure verb until nothing remains
to move or be moved but movement itself
smeared into time

and the manner of the turning, the turning
of the turning
the sentences disappearing
echoes lurking in a phrase
(words never before seen
troop past my windows)
and I am nowhere to be found

Anything can happen
(and usually does).

Whispers from a library. Written for the tenth anniversary of the Waiheke Library building, 2024

Every day is an adventure. The adventure of all time. Line up! Line up! White knuckle rafting through seas of fire. Villains and their heroes. Shoot the tube! Ride the curl! Every day, a miracle might happen; the marvelous might open out like a good story, shadows cave in, the magician might tip his hat, the maestro take a bow, violins quiver their dying fall. You remain upright even in the midst of war. The tables of abundance. Emergence. Radiance. Music is spherical. Like science, it begins with imagination and ends in mystery, begins in mystery and ends in wonder. The universe has no edge therefore no centre. You are at the centre. The centre is here. The centre is a library. Hear the words whisper and shout, gambol and play. They all have something to say. On their spines they cry. Like lovers they open, softly, to a lover's eye, while the pages flick by, tickety-tick. Universes come and go. Tickety-tick.

Every day is a blank page, a tabula rasa, for the universe to inscribe its will, and inscribe it again in flowing lines. Lines between lines. Lines after lines. Unbroken wholeness. It haunts us. Your will is another matter. You can barely inscribe your will on the flesh. Flesh goes its own way, cleaves to itself, cleaves to the grave. A bell swings a forgotten morning. We need not want. We need not wait. We can stop the rot. It's all open ended; nothing is determined, not even the end of the sentence (can you finish what you started?). There is airy talk of destiny. You never know, people say, you never know (they always say it with a knowing look), and of course you never do. Anything and everything can happen (the art always wins). The moment is exploding feathers. Hear the music of sad trombones, of planetary loops, of wilting custard squares, of feedback dances. Of rising seas and burning skies. That's what matters.

Anything can happen in life, especially nothing, but don't be fooled by your boredom. Nothing is a nothing word. It is not guaranteed; you can't rely on it. You can't put a condo up on it. I wouldn't put my money on a horse that runs backwards. Nothing doesn't last. Nothing turns inside out. Something crops up. The blank page is never enough. There is a big bang. There are lines. The deadpan sky is scribbled in blue. Time arrives complete with streamers. History pulls a face. The corn ripens. Nothing can come of nothing, the Fool says to Lear, but something always comes, even of nothing. Out of the nothing comes the something, out of the incomprehensibly long night. Think of it! The boys might pick up their toys and go home. The rich might support a living wage for all. The homeless might be homed. The homophobe might embrace their brother. The sky might turn upside down. Blessings pour out. Paint might run on beatific faces eager for the carnival. People might wake up honest, and start weeping, and start laughing, and start weeping again. Meet in the street and laugh and weep. Tickety teep. They exchange eyes. Children sing with their feet. Their faces are smeared with ash. Bones surrender their memories. Incandescence rules, planets form; it's heartbreaking. Heartstopping. Worldthrobbing. Everybody is beside themselves. Everybody is at sixes and sevens. They cannot bury their dead fast enough. Where there are no feet there are no paths. Where there are no paths there are no songs. Where there are no songs there is no life. The moment has no feet therefore time has no paths. The smooth flow of time gets fractured by the years and the fears and the changing gears.

The safety pins holding your insanity in place slip open. They just do. That's the grace of it. Fatality takes a back seat. The world comes right on in. Your insanity loses its privilege. Your madness comes unstuck, and you learn how to tame sleep. Decoherence is reversed. Sanity has a chance to do some breaking and entering. Lawyers drop their briefs. Banks start accepting prayers as collateral. Prayers start getting answered. They call it Resonant Energy Transfer. RET. It happens in the blink of an eye. Your long-lost lover turns up at the door with shining eyes and a choice of pasts. Your pet algae starts doing yoga. Your phone plays hell with a big stick. Your social media feeds consume themselves and spit you out. These algorithms of discontent. You abandon your inventions. Columns of the dispossessed trudge from the city, ruled by hunger, thirst and heat. Garbage collects at the bottom of the ocean. Micro-plastics collect everywhere, even to the farthest reaches of your soul. Grief can no longer hide its face. Grief finds its face. Grief contains multitudes. Your poems begin to replicate, if they don't already. They are beside themselves, poor copies of each other. What we wanted each other to be. Your poems leave home in search of the good life. They all weep the same tears. We awaken from the dream of the dark forest where we have for too long slept. We make room for our frailty. Our dreams do not outlive us. We can do nothing but fade into history. It all went by so fast. On the moment of her death, beloveds, there was an odour, as if a perfect rose had passed through the room.

Everything that can happen does happen as your hands get older. Veins happen. Skin happens. Belly and thigh happen. Feet splay and splodge. Grace descends. Your eyes go free. Your legs go happy-go-lucky. Your shadow grows short. Your breath arrives from the far side of conversation. Every passing moment is an adventure, the outcome up for grabs. Hell, it could all go the other way. It could turn on a dime. Kickback. Reverse order. Feedback loops of language. Tickety-tickety. Lift the horizontal, flatten the curve, shoot the tube again. The crumbling edges. That sinking feeling never goes away, beloveds. Words come apart at the seams. The books cry out in their dreams. Language is never at rest. Words grow from the inside. Follow the floating feather. The news is there in black and white. The pages flick by. Tickety-tick, tickety-tick.

What happens doesn't have to make sense. It is under no obligation; sense comes at a price. The price may be too high; only a fool would pay. Mosquitoes arrive to teach me compassion. That makes sense to them. Clouds of blood part to show the way; the promised land right before your eyes, from the river to the sea let your words run free. On the fringes of the night you fight back tears over which you have no control. Here is the light that was once hidden away. Here is the neglected darkness. Here are the children with eyes cracked like empty dinner plates. Here, the blackened sunflower turns to light.

You never know your luck in a big city, my father used to say. He said that because we were country people, where luck was hard to find. You might find luck on a street corner. A stranger slips you a get out of jail free card, and you know you are alive. Your casket springs open. The hunt is on. That's luck. That's serendipity in your eyes. Potentially there's no end to it, to what could happen, the sky's the limit, they say. What they mean is that the sky's no limit. Everything you can imagine is imaginable in phonemes. Bliss rules. Every streak of light and shadow is anchored to the facades of buildings. To the liminal. Dust rises from the end of the broom. See the dance of the feather duster and the fly swat. A little girl with a bob goes by on a bicycle. The belt on her schoolbag catches the light and flings it. Traffic lights blink with somnambulant persistence. Night arrives on the wings of soft moths. It all happens at a speed beyond sensation. Tickety-tick. Pages purr. Histories blur. Everything is taking place in its designated space. It is here, the momentary place from which we speak and honour words and have words to spare.

Anything can happen.

It just did.

1st January

The young poet referred to is Li He (790 - 816) who wrote the lines 'Need further proof?/ Here's a man raging at the wall while carving his questions to heaven' (Stay At Home Today Pilgrim). These lines were picked up by Roger Waters of Pink Floyd, 'Witness the man who raves at the wall/Making the shape of his questions to Heaven ('Set the controls for the heart of the sun,' 1968).

is just another day
in a year of days
another dawn in a year of dawns
prizing open the mind with the same force
gentle yet implacable
like running water
like passing time
like old sweet songs
like a knife through butter
like a smile of love
like these well-worn words
near worn out
pause at the threshold

can we survive another spin of the wheel?

nobody I know expects things to get better
just because a page has turned
because we have kissed the perfumed morning rain

and made amends with the past
the news is in the wind
the writing's on the wall where the poet
first inscribed his complaints to heaven
the heavens turned silent
gargoyles glared
flowers burst into flame on their stems
and the poet died young heaving up

his lungs
but maybe I don't know the right people
the people in the know
the smart money with the shapely legs
botoxed brows
and shrewd investments

his words remain, the complaints survive
the tears still fall
the moving walls
dividing night from day, year from year
haven't crumbled with the centuries
but live in the mind where they separate
self from self from self, dawn from dawn
new years and familiar fears
old Halloween faces
and three-legged races

I thought there might be a fresh start
but instead wake with the same old ache
the same old fake, and can feel my bones
in my balls

as the same old forever war drags on
with all the usual excuses

I look up into the sky for just another moment
in a life composed of many such moments
(the lightest touch of the brush)
to see the clouds lighten, hear the tūī chatter
the day bark, a horn bray

as the last all-night parties wind down
and tomatoes begin to ripen
for just another day
in a year of days

Onetangi new year: salute to the sun

two sail boats overlap, briefly
the horizon
folded from end to end like a paper yacht
one scrubby line
rolling out the hills of Thompson's Point
for everybody's delectation

all the ripple and slide you could desire
and then some occasional kelp, protoplasmic blobs
with nowhere else to go

I don't know if the shape we took
was ever a choice so much as
the way it fell out
the way the cookie crumbled
the loaves and the fishes
what the body sought
fashioned by that ocean
into the lineaments of desire

someone's meditating, someore's doing yoga
someone's jumping for a ball
someone's pretending that no one's dying

others step up into the sky to catch the sun
before it turns into day
weaving straw into gold

the girl with the red shoes
keeps on dancing until her feet bleed

what could be lighter than the dotterel
skipping over the sand
at the beginning of the world
funnier than bloated sparrows on breadcrumb patrol
sadder than an old sweet song
more vivid than this wrinkled old one
still searching for their Goldilocks moment
amid shards of orange cloud

that jogger with long legs makes short work
of a beach run, like a sailboard slicing through
the years
gives rise to floating
lifted from above as the kite fills with wind
lifting the sailboard
keeping it alive, keeping the
weave of day, a scented breeze
just as it is
in the moment of suspension
when the orca leaps

three red kayaks belly up, sunbathing
there are enough words to go around
enough of a circle to make a day
enough lines for a world
we don't need much, just the thread
now much faded
just the convergence
much anticipated

we pray for the indulgence of the gods
maybe one more year, we say,
just to see what happens
we'll be very good, we'll keep quiet
and very still
keep a clean nose
no one will hear us
we will hear no evil and speak no evil
war won't come our way

pingao curls up through the sand
seeking purchase
ready for the swelling tide

the rock we're standing on should be good
for another thousand years
under the ocean
where monstrous beings walk

the old year is still in our arms
but sleeping

at the turn of a thought, the wind changes
now we see it
from the other side of the crease
beyond the gutter
hear it between the floorboards
your sands now drift

your sketch a few wisps of pencil lead
lines that cannot land
but only stretch forward

blood transfusion

I come across in a trickle
from two dimensions to three

slow awakening of the veins
the rowdy world before me

arisen
from the pale land

out of the gray to colour
line and form

things regain their shadows
the sound of rushing water

the bridge that runs across
the lair of vigilant trolls

what was blurry, becomes sharp
what was hidden, shows a face

the fixed bursts into movement
the stagnant quickens

your full name and date of birth, please
the nurse says

have you already forgotten? I say

the promise

I waited by the corner of the sky
as it grew light
(the moon took an exit, stage left)
but you didn't emerge
as the children had written
in their luscious crayon stories

the elements all stayed in character
and there were no exciting turning points
although plenty of people were carried out
under white sheets for no good reason

I waited by the old, hollow pūriri tree
(Vitex lucens)
where the kids used to play hide and seek
slipping between their years
bits of coloured paper in their mouths
on the tip of their tongues
the promise in their hearts

the most solemn promise
swear-to-god-and-hope-to-die
kind of promise
in the kneeling hours

the earth stood still
everything flew upward, unconstrained

as gravity broke open
the cow jumped over the moon
and we grew older and sought each other out
in the dead of night, flying

through astronomical space
through the ceremonial dark
asking for no more than we were given
(the children grew like buttercups
in the cracks between the stones)

I wrote a few lines, if anything
to relieve the heart of its mysteries
of its groping, and
with each line a little more of the world
came into view
until the story made itself felt

but you didn't rise like the morning mist
or open like a rose
or declare yourself like a sacred scroll
(meanwhile, people kept dying
that's what they did, gave up the ghosts
which wandered through half-remembered stories
looking for themselves)

I waited by the corner of the sky
where the shadows gathered
(enter moon, stage right)
but there was no sign
or counter-sign
of you

Fairy Summer

the night's not dark
it's velvet

sleep slips down the throat
like an oyster

dreams come and go
with a hectic temporality

dawn arrives on the wings
of soft moths

the sky's not light
it's textured

I am a swarm
(with thanks to Carlo Rovelli)

I am not an entity
I am a swarm
I am a throng
a scatterment

as our present seethes
with traces of our past
I abound

we are histories
of ourselves

I am the traces
of the phrases I am writing

I am the distances
I once travelled
in hope and fear

I am the layers
of what I have read

I am what I have heard
and written
loved, despised and grieved

I am the faces
I cannot forget

I am the mystery
of my brew

I am my own
passing parade

I am the one
who has just composed
the sentence
I am now completing

I am this long
ongoing novel
word by word

I am the impossible fairy tale
my mother once read to me

I am the echo
which fades away

if all this vanished
would I still be?

I am nothing but
the memory
that solders together
the processes
of which we are made

scattered across time

Mangawhai

it's been a long time, as the dragon's tail
is long
the sky coral, the wind keen
the windchime hangs from a thread
of wood and shell
making a hollow sound

the estuary is carefully sculptured by generations of
like-minded waves, the
sand dunes on the seaward side look as if they could
wash away
with the passing thought

the sea is a deep jade, the sand a soft blonde
the black dog with white feet
makes ghost tracks on the wet shore

that's a given, the rest will follow fast
the headland will gleam like polished bone
the clouds will choose a broody grey for this moment
history will stay buried, a kite makes a red half
moon
in a morning sky

the sun will appear just in time to catch
a white-fronted tern on the swing

Mangawhai 2

there's a rock shaped like a fish's tail
frosted by bird droppings
disappearing into a child's book

a group of swaggering boys with voices
that blow about

a yellow backpack abandoned at the high tide mark
has a story to tell

a rocky island with bleak crags
is wreathed by screaming gulls

a long breakwater made of dark stones

we lie back on the Muehlenbeckia
as if we had all the time in the world

a little rain falls out of a blue sky

Halloween

branches fall from the trees
for no apparent reason
but to crack open the quiet
leaves fly upward with eerie calm

cats leave their eyes behind in the dark
turning the asphodels yellow

the dead go for a stroll
their eyes peeled for the main chance

a teddy bear nailed to a tree
still struggles to grin
while grandma's gone with a song
and left her bones behind
to rattle in the wind

on this hellbound train
the sky rises and fades with hectic regularity
the years have been spirited away
on the back of a three-faced demon
that knows your secret places
your other faces
and doesn't give a damn

beware the jabberwok, my friend
beware the jubjub bird

hobgoblins can be glimpsed
slipping between their spells
as the moon rises amid tides
of purple blood

a jack of spades sits on a letterbox
boy, does he have a deal for you

birds roost in the sky
their claws holding onto giddy spaces

the sky is carved into a single dark mask

I think I'm coming down with something
I can't taste the world, I can't
smell the roses and I can't
think straight

words break open and reveal
their empty centres like yawning graves

or like children playing dress-ups and painting
their faces
with clown smiles
putting on their witches' hats
as the hour grows late

these words can't trick or treat
or promise them anything
other than their phantasms

it's all the magician's illusion

when midnight strikes
we will turn into owls
the moment of truth will come

time, now, to put on the music
suck on a red-spiraled lollipop
and haunt the streets

on reading Mary Oliver's 'When Death Comes'

suddenly I can't bear to look
at anything I've set down
it's all gone lame and fails to walk
on its own two feet

I want to go back and unravel it all
line by line
cluster by cluster
and disperse it to the four directions
and directions
that haven't been invented yet
except in fairy tales

or better, bury them
with the ribs of old books
in an unmarked grave
after a hasty prayer and quick libation

'I want to step through the door full of curiosity,
wondering:
what is it going to be like, that cottage of
darkness?'

my lines lie, awkward, flat and imprecise
poke them and they wriggle a little
but that's all

they have no flair
they don't take wing the way they might
across the gutter of the page
beyond the margins
and into the open air

they won't make a welcome mat
for the threshold
of that dark cottage

'and I think of each life as a flower, as common
as a field daisy, and as singular'

the poem is a lot nicer before it's written
when on the verge of
hovering luminous
and undeclared
that inchoate excitement
that precedes the act
before anything has to sprawl
ungainly and graceless
and finally revealed
petals askew

'and each name a comfortable music in the mouth,
tending, as all music does, toward silence'

these are not soaring syllables
but wordles, uncomfortable by nature
to rhyme with nurdles, the nasties

that pile up in dusty corners
war-torn courtyards

and places of natural wonder beloved of birds
and creatures that know how to sing

'I want to say all my life
I was a bride married to amazement.
I was the bridegroom, taking the world into my arms'

I long now for nothing but a clean screen
a nascent sky
an unbudded rose
and the long, polished rush of a Mary Oliver poem

Te Toki

this spider web has ensnared
the fluffy olearia seeds
(Olearia traversiorum)
holding them in quivering suspension
as a scattering, a smattering
like tiny velvety insects

we are on the edge of the wetland
which is the edge of the ocean
which is the edge of once upon a time
hurtling through space
gyrating around the black spider hole
at the centre of the galaxy

we can hear the heron's tapering cry
but we can't spot it
no matter how quietly we sit

tall kānuka and pōhutukawa overhang
a still mud pool
low tide
bristling with mangrove sticks
breathing
the humid air of high summer

when the rains come
the kānuka sway stiffly
and groan
while the mud rushes and bubbles
and the leaves of the olearia
go into a frantic confabulation
as the lines of the web blur
and the seeds purr
and the spider stirs

and we become that memory

Owhanake Bay

you can see the remains of the old wharf
where they loaded cattle
for shipment to Auckland
looking for the good life

broken toothed snippets of kauri
encrusted with ocean
rusty as iron
jagged as oyster shells

you can see the scars on the hillsides
from the slash n' burn
burn n' slash
in the quest for cash

only in the steepest valleys can you find
fragments of the old forest
still harbouring memories of an older stillness
a forgotten inwardness

a leaf and a sky from ancient Gondwanaland
and the festive cry
of a multitude of birds

Thompson's Point at sunrise

out in the bay
there's a light still sparking from the tip of a
mast
like a seagull about to fly
like a fairy on top of a Christmas tree
like a semaphoring angel
like the spark of a heart that never ceased
to beat
no matter how long the night

there's a creamy toetoe feeling to the rocking wind
a cruise ship suspended in the clouds over Auckland
intermingled streaks of sea and sky
a lone hawk like a floating eye

there's a cool wind playing at the nearest bay
for free
colours splashed over the world from above
partying light, chasing day

I've tried to talk myself out of pretty much
everything
I'd talked myself into

an arduous undertaking
a habit I can't seem to shake

the hospitality of the heavens is not that far away
swallows dip and glide across the green hillside
here's an invitation you can't refuse
a call to play

I walk along the track
always the same track
the muehlenbeckia follows me seeking
quantum entanglements
I lost something back there in the snarl of time

returning home, I pick the last of the figs
from the neighbours' tree
for free
and fill my pockets

if there's something out there
(an anything kind of something)
galloping my way on hooves of wind
it might find me at breakfast
quite calm
with tea over toast

Poukaraka Flats

taking a short cut across Poukaraka Flats
to the beach
I'm reluctant to disturb two dotterels
who look like little beetling lumps of sand
fluffed up by the wind

I find a seat and look out over Rocky Bay
with its little clutter of yachts at anchor
their masts hardly stirring
wondering where the years went
or if they ever were in the first place
having come and gone like a whisper
of breath
like a rumour of mountains
passing by

the past is conjectural, the body
makes itself felt in the sunlight and tides
of living moments

I begin to sense what lift off
might feel like
                    the sudden cessation of gravity

wordless, one wave beyond
the ache of the world
the dotterel takes wing

a magpie in its severe black and white
reminds me of my childhood home
before colour arrived
going to Birdlings Flat, Te Mata Hapuku
looking for polished gemstones
quartz, agate and jasper
in which obdurate colour was born
and which now take brief solidity
in this passing flush of words
the magpie's chortle

whatever I thought I held
never was
what I imagined
whatever that was
but slipped this way and that
into and out of the field
on a wing and sigh

while sitting here, distracted by words
trapped in amber
the tide has quietly occupied the slip of beach
I walked along to get here

to return to my starting point
my point of origin
my source
I'll have to go the long way around

Nelson, April 2 – 7

black curtains hide the window to my room
what lies behind
is way above our pay grade, beloved
off the charts
and into the blue yonder

something is coming into focus
all by itself, without our help
reluctant to show its face
coy as young love, shy as dawn

listen hard enough and you'll hear
far off
the breaking of chains
the loosening of light

*

portal

it's a rough old farm gate
made of wire and wooden planks
with rusty iron hinges
and a simple loop of rope
to hitch it to a fence post
sitting in the middle of nowhere
covered in weeds
overhung by young kānuka, vigourous

in their viridescent faith
and lit by spider webs as sticky as memory
where the praying mantis chants
you will find me, one arm resting
on my time-bleached lines
while the gate holds me up

no longer does it keep anything in
or out
but the echo of its intention
is there, in the construction
the oblong and the diagonals
a Platonic form with rusty nails
and a colonial air

if I push open the gate, if I venture through
if I pass from one footstep to the next
from one innocuous patch of grass
to another
into the world of the Mad King
the Jealous Queen
or the Death Star
will the sun still shine on the faces
of those I love
will day follow night in ancient procession
as was written
will the paddock beyond still gleam
with mud and green
in a place called home

will plantain and golden rod still hold
to the verges

and will this same heart still thump
in the chest that houses it
and the words that shape it
at the edge of the creek
where dragonflies float like little UFOs
midges skitter
like children out of school
and water wrinkles like the skin of an old person

will the gate remain
half open, at least
for me to beat
a hasty retreat?

*

there's a church without a name
just around the corner
from where I'm staying in Collingwood Street

it's all boarded up and long abandoned
grass grows long and lank
around the broken steps that lead
to the locked door

but the bell tolls at random
moments
a mellow sound, not to call
the faithful to prayer or sweetly mark the hours
but apparently from sheer joy
a celebration of its own mystery
choosing to ring out
whenever the spirit takes it

*

willow walk

I want to walk as far upstream
as my feet will carry me

turning back
there's always that moment of regret

I'm not looking for the source
exactly
or the fairy castle

I just want to see
what's around
the next corner

*

perhaps tonight
when the day has shed its colours
we will be again
in that way of being
at ease and in delight

ready to open the book of words
and find ourselves
where we once were
as if for the first time

Matariki

I didn't know what to say
my mouth had lost its way and there were oblique
bits
that didn't fit
other bits
too rough for the tongue

everybody was on edge, stars quick to fade
the planet had its hottest week
in a hundred and fifty thousand years
but everyone had their own business to mind
and dragons had their gold
to hoard

the authorities call for calm
while the situation calls for panic

my love brought me a new year kiss
on dawn's spreading wing
I admire the sky's pale orange
(the merest hint of colour)
and the fit of her kiss on my skin

I'm not going anywhere
I have an aneurysm which at any moment
might burst
so every step becomes a prayer

even if you're not religious
someone is walking over your grave
in the torrid heat

I don't know what to say
there are places words can't go
however hard they try
merely bring us to the threshold
the first line of the fairy tale

beyond that, it's just
a matter of time

The Dreaming Dead

zombie rhymes

the dreaming dead
don't know where they're going
or where they've been
what they've done
what they've seen
or when they last fed

having forgotten just about everything
their own bloody footprints
the lives they led
the blood they shed

the loves they abandoned
their resonant houses
their echoing skies
their bleeding eyes

the mindless war
the seeping sore
the dream that never ends

they are driven by an insensate purpose
that attaches their eyeballs to their hind brains
that animates their limbs
that pushes them to take another
stinking breath
that reeks of death

theirs is a eyeless hunger
they can't leave behind
a distillation of torment
a crackling backbone
the long groan

they are our shadow selves
regressing, reaching
for an impossible blessing

Sunday 31ˢᵗ Dec 2023

I seem to come from far away
earth's boneless voice
a shiftless dust

after a lifetime of sifting through syllables
suddenly there's nothing to say
nothing that could change the world
or lick the wound
no uplifting call

cruelty and lies rule the mirror world
I dare not enter
the fact-free zone where shadows
take substance
flesh turns transparent
on the spin of coin
and mass graves are dug for the children
who have no escape

is that my face?

I wake up on the last day of the year
feeling powdery and heady
invisible
and ransack my despair for leavings of hope
in the moment to moment, the moment
of play

the blind shuffle
in search of a blessing
where the blessings have been shed

I pass, voiceless, through walls of air
and cunning words, wanting
to keep my breath steady
my heart ready
open for business
on another Monday

not just yet

I felt a tap on the shoulder
and heard a silky voice which said
haven't you had enough of this world of folly
war, weariness and woe
aren't you in fact ready to go?

oh no, I said, you see
I'm just too jolly comfortable
and well fed
(so far)
sitting in my garden
watching the weeds grow

undercover

In those distant days, beloved
madness was let loose upon the earth
grief followed fast behind
rivers took to the sky
deserts walked on bony feet
birds fell dead out of the air
and graves couldn't keep up with
all the bodies

people saw all kinds of crazy shit
maybe a mouse nibbling at the moon
maybe the flying pigs the evil witch of the west
had given wings
and launched into the air
to cause narrative chaos
at the intersections of thought
neural gridlock

some saw reptiles walking about
in human form, sneaky shapeshifters
with clawed feet
or saw mothers tearing off the faces of babies
to wear over their own
and sucking out their vital essence
with plastic straws

people lost the power to distinguish the nightmare
from daily life, beloved
as one turned into the other

and people turned into their dopplegangers
as old grifters polished up their pitch
and the black pit yawned

then the guns came out and people shot the stories
out of each other's heads
children cried, and ran around looking
for bits of language which still worked
a hey-diddle-diddle
ding-dong-daddy
and a vigorous see-saw Margery door
Jackie shall have a new master
he shall earn but a penny a day, because
he can't work any faster

death and mayhem couldn't stop the stories
which grew madder with every passing hour
unhinging reason
putting in its place a screaming face
and putting love on the line

many of us
became refugees
carrying with us other kinds of stories
true, warm-hearted things
that connected to other
warm-hearted things
whispered to each other in the silence
when silence fell
and under the cover of darkness
walked the words through

after

after the make-believe
comes the sausage sizzle
in the demesne of the rich
where atonement comes
on the tip of skewer
with dead meat and
lots of tomato sauce and
bright laughter

go north, go south
if you're bait, there's no
getting off the hook
no escaping the gaping mouth

when the ferris wheel stops
you can kiss goodbye to the fairground
the foreground
the playground
the swinging lanterns of the light house
the screaming and clatter
the shrieks of the girls, the hoarse cries of the
boys
the chatter of fireworks
love will keep hold of your hand
even in the crazy house
where people chase their minds
from one mad idea to the next
and the walking dead are all puppets

go north, go south
with only poor devices
there's no holding back the ghost train
or the amazing vanishing man
except love's laughter

you, who never recognized yourself
in the bent mirror
still, you heard her song
you remembered the words
you found your voice

after the candy-floss photograph
and the ice-cream moments
the imperceptible loss of years
will blur the image
steal the image away

bow north, bow south
when you've finished with all of that
bowing
the odds turn against you
the numbers run dry
the ducks won't die
the give-away teddy bears lose their smiles

those detached clown heads that turn back and forth
with their mouths open
are swallowing the sky

and your money
in accordance with their own mechanism
after the sausage sizzle
and a couple of beers
it feels like home time
and you're grateful to be back
in your own time and place, among things
you recognize, and people who say 'hello'

light frames the window
where the organ grinder takes a bow
and his monkey puts down her violin

go north, go south
and all the destinations between
the days are back on the job
and so are you

waiting

we waited for years and nobody came
we sat at the weeping tables
by the sad windows
with dusty spiderwebs
silent doors and fallen hearts
in barren kitchens
vacant living rooms, abandoned
bedrooms
and nobody came
even the dead stayed away
on other business

we were like a couple of clowns
in a play

the years were empty
the hills were empty
the sky was empty
the birds were emptied of their song
the plate licked clean
the bones put to rest
histories made vacant
time dethroned

when we open the door
cross the threshold
our hearts agape
all we want
is for something new to happen

tīpuna push back

coming up to the new year I find
with age
the barrier between matter and mind
body and spirit, present and past
has worn thin
powdery as moths' wings
as my ancestors crowd in
clamouring at the threshold
remonstrating and mewling
throwing their weight around
those ungrateful dead

flesh, it's flesh they want, and
breath, fiery breath

they wail and shout
full of piss and wind and rage
and glory
death takes the moral high ground
waves a bony finger

you, yes you, rash and righteous ones
with the blood of the land on your hands
and a tongue of ashes
what can you tell me that's sound?

begone, unquiet spirits!
let me sleep, let me know
a moment's peace
liberation from the grind of mind
(the mind of grind)
let a ceasefire of the soul
take hold
put history to rest
before we all go down
in flame and dirty smoke

I'm tired of tossing and turning
on a grid of fire
your raucous voices in my head
your gaping mouths, your once-were-wise
your double bind
you've had your say
your hour to strut and fret
upon your stage
the least you could do
you fractious crew
is stay good and dead

Leila gives me a drop of scotch thistle essence
the remedy for dealing with crybullies
and know-it-alls
like you
to help throw you out
banish you and vanish you
so I can find my way

however ham-fisted
into the new dawn
rinsed wide
and emptied

find the joy I knew when I was a boy
unencumbered, unalloyed
as the year turns
and music pours forth
and hands are joined
to hands
on a fresh and glad day

hold it right there

I tried to make time, couldn't
squeeze it in, somehow
between all the other bits
that needed squeezing in
the cries and whispers
honour and betrayal
a broken trail
through the ruins of hillsides
and vacant chronicles

places where the dead dream free
and life struggles to get a look in

I was oppressed by daily concerns
stuck on this fuckup or that fuckup
or somebody else's fuck up
time went south on doubt, fear, chagrin
mortification, panic
and all the rest of the razzle-dazzle
of discombobulation

you can't make time
time makes you
Jiminy Cricket says

so I didn't see it coming
couldn't see it coming
… the burst fruit, the jab of light
the coming on of the world

it may come

it may come from a busy street full of clatter
or morning rain shining gray
or the pine-needle hush of waking
from the rush of a crowded dream
on a crowded train
heading for the mirrored city
that rises up in the shadow lands
of the long wail

it may come in the middle of a conversation
between words, on top of them
from a hollow ribcage, or
swarming page
anywhere we might meet
for a moment of love

it may come on a floating feather or
iron hailstones, flash floods
a crashing hard drive, or
your most secret pity

in soft-sheeted love or angular rage
reconciled or forbidden
in water or air, earth or fire
it may come
first nowhere
then somewhere

then everywhere
on everybody's lips
dank and sweet

and when it comes, you will
not be caught
off balance
and you will know the place
for the first time

the invisible swarm

we never saw them coming, he said
one moment we were alone, the next
they were all around us, amongst us
the air was full of them
flies collected at the corners of our eyes
our heads became unscrewed
our limbs deserted

people died standing up, or walking
they kept walking until they realized
they had forgotten how to breathe
kept walking until there was no more road

some had names for them, some
didn't bother, others didn't get the time
their mouths too full of flies

bodies filled the trenches
as fast as they could be dug
by masked teams working in relays
all through the night

nobody knew when it would end
but a few, as always, closed their eyes
hung on
and waited it out

we must make way for

there's a special hell reserved
for old phone numbers

moist notebooks
unopened letters from IRD
dust balls under the bed
and iron fingernails

forgotten things may come back to life
that's not necessarily desirable
or suitable for a healthy imagination
let the dead bury
their memories

forget, forgot, forgotten
a natural conjugation
that fades us into
a bungy jump to oblivion
a circumlocutious sleep
an awakening hunger

the afterlife as a pinball machine
time as a sleepwalker

'we are never more than one step ahead
of the posse,' my father would say
those relentless horsemen

from cities of fire and blood
hunting him down through ordinary streets
and bank balances

he knew that one day they would get him
and nail him to the wall

there are good reasons for forgetting

ghosts don't belong in the sunlight

(pedestrians remain committed to their roles
windows open and shut, horns blare, children skip
on their way to school)

some memories you can live with
some are a danse macabre
dressed in costumes
from all walks of life

(sunrays pass right through
leaving no trace on the glass)

we must make way for
the star and the plough
the word and the sign
melody's rise and fall

lie down in our sturdy graves
and leave behind
what has to be left

to the general mystery
time twisting our thumbs

we return by the way we came
through the house of dawns
knowing the place by its landmarks
white crosses and slabs of stone
fat little sparrows made of fire
plaster gnomes with pointy heads
gardens made of vertical and horizontal
lines
the croak of the kākā
the wheeze of desire

your cards are stacked away in their box
face down
their divinations collapse with impossible softness
and speed
we can't hear a sound

collapse, collapsed, collapsing
we can see the marks on the stone
where they passed
etchings on the shell
the careless fall of bird cries

you, there, escape the story
(it was never yours)
go off on your own
sing children's rhymes
dance on donkey feet

cultivate non-Euclidian spaces
on the curve of the lily
live dangerously

only after dark do you discover
your boundaries
and boundaries that are no longer
you

there is somebody behind me
a creature of some sort
another sort of somebody
who lives in stolen faces
who has to highball their pain
who makes no eye contact with the world
who whimpers and whinges
treading in my steps

it's important to forget them so that
we may, in turn, be forgotten
and the real thing, the true article
can take place everywhere
at once

sleep when you die

at the end of the day
there's not much left

everybody's tired
the booze has run out
and the drugs are running low

everybody feels as if they're in
a Salvador Dali painting

yet nobody's too keen to run off
to their bed of nails
and no one's asking for the moon on a stick

no one wants to lead the way
through the ruins of war
on bleeding feet

we sit around with sounds coming out
of our mouths, some bright and sharp
some slow and lackadaisical

which quiver and burst in the air
where they leave momentary wet fragments
that fall to the floor

it won't be long now
before our liminal angels
with their lustrous voices
and their enfolding, will arrive
with their promised gift

Wild Clay

roots

what we seek
in the sunless, dank earth
the wild clay
and bunched rocks
with our multitudinous tentacles
and mycorrhizal extensions
is not nutriment only
or the history of the earth
but connections
infinite connections
and a vision so bright
it might inspire
branches far above us to reach
for the freedom of the sky

love poem

I have been here before
at this exact same spot
at the exact same time
when I was wooing love
wooing the soft sigh

and I swear the same waves
were sliding over the same hot sand
under the same water colour washed sky
the same black beer swirling in rhyme
with the wild, sticky clay

it's just like coming home

it is an illusion, however fond
every wave is different from every other
every sky breaks new
and I've never seen a beer last
beyond the bottom of the glass

although I could swear
these are the very same lips
I kissed, and kissed
all those years ago

point of view

from this field of yellow flowers
the mountain looks far off

while it is but a stone's throw away

from the mountain, the field looks
like a crumpled handkerchief
rolled in an artist's palette

while it is but a wing tip away

from the night's silence, noisy dawn
is a mere conjecture

while it is already at hand

and love, flirting lovelessness
seems doomed never to arrive

yet it has already taken your heart

rear view

what looks far off
can suddenly be
right on top of you

there, the last birds
against the darkening sky
the sky is sweet
like a watercolour painting

in the distance I see thunderheads
while the hand of love
is in my hand
and what looks far is suddenly
very close

you would never know
the moment of its coming
through the rear-view mirror
where the world comes up
and passes by
and the hand of love
will never leave my hand
even while the birds are in
the sky's hand of love
where they are borne up gently
and what is in the rear- view mirror
is no longer in the rear-view mirror

the hand of love is on my shoulder
and that love will be there
whichever side of the sky I am on
and whenever I fly with the birds
through the softness and the darkness

the secret

the outer petals have curled back
and are going brown at the edges

they open to the rose's dark, scarlet furnace
each petal aflame

truly, I am growing a new skin over her memory
and living
every declared moment through
as if it were my last

the survivor

I thought I could see my way through
the murk and the blood
the right and the wrong
the then and the now
the quick and the dead
the loved and the loveless

I thought I could handle the jandal

like navigating by the stars
I just had to keep looking up
divining the shape of the night
while my legs carried on
by themselves

it didn't work that way
there were no stars
there was no up, no sideways
no back and forth
no waka of endless night
no wheel or plough
no ley lines of song
no take or give

so I looked to you, old friend
with your kindly hands
your bag of sticks to throw

your runes to trace
to find a contour, a future
scratchings on stone
configurations of mud
pictures pretty as water lilies
a half-forgotten face
and a stillborn line

I thought I could see my way through
to where I once was
before all this started
imagining stars, imagining directions
imagining an ocean
where the gods live
just to the outside of time
and the sunny side of love

the coming of age

I stood by the midnight path
after midnight had gone
after the breezes had faded
and the faces had gone home

waiting for the night to settle
waiting for the patupaiarehe to arrive
the people before the people
children of atua
out of the mists and shadows
with their songs of stone
their spirit mythologies
and fables of love

I have seen them, but briefly
and sideways
I saw one once, a woman with a fluid body
huia wings
and a cannibal smile

I know from the tick-tock of the clock
inside the crocodile's belly
that I don't have much time
to set things straight
and neither does the world

In the dreams of the dispossessed
dawn never comes
as if the light of a new day
is nothing but a fairy tale
and even the first cracks in the horizon
are not enough to break
our enchantment

we the children lost to time, we
take to the streets
hurling our multi-coloured streamers
into the open graves of the land
and sing our hearts out

the shift

you can always see a familiar place
from an unfamiliar angle
and get to know it all over again
its new topographies
its soft and swell
the chorus of touch
whole or part
love and lorn

the shapes are different, colours revised
intentions faded
shadows displaced, transfigured
figures transposed, nothing
holding still

the way the bay moves around the eye
the headlands shift east to west
on their gyroscope
the lone pine reels on its axis
or leans at a different angle into
the same wind

the sky uptilted
the ocean swapping places with the sky
the gulls swapping places with the stars
desire swapping places with
desire

it doesn't matter that I've seen it all
from other angles, this way
or that, as it always looks new
with every turn of the head
every forward, headlong movement
eye-switch

every shift of the heart

leapfrog

words play leapfrog
with the world
and the world plays
leapfrog
with your heart

over they go
still on their feet
bouncing light
down the street
near and far

the cow jumps over the
silver spoon
the baby cries
for no other reason

words play leapfrog
with the bouncing light
(I have saved this road for you)
and played leap-
frog, leap

with the years

Spellbreaker

spellbreaker

I have heard the music
of planetary collisions
the sigh of stars
the thunder of gravity sinks
the quivering string

before radiance was invented
and the bow of time was bent

felt the grainy softness of the infinity beach
how the light grows heavy
when the earth stands still and the sun
doesn't move
and nobody knows which way to turn
because directions have got lost

felt the ache in the taut muscles of the archer
who must hold his pose
forever
at the point of release
the falcon's eye

the desired explosion is movement
tender, spectacular birth
set in motion, ghostly luminescence
turned dervish in the light

the earth tipping into the sun
headlong
across the spiral arm

the arrow buried deep
in the event horizon

when things fall

when things fall, they fall
fast
and they fall together
and away
into some new complicated ruin

at the same time, triggered
by unseen signals
from the galaxy's heart
the long word
and
sentences that don't yet exist
or may never exist
become my shadow
I hear them whisper

I may escape this page
and clusters of syllables
heartbreak and love
that travel impossible distances
bend around verbs and nouns
and remain unseen
for no sentence can complete
me

not easy

it's not easy to see these things
in their true light

even distant stars are cloaked
in thought and desire

north and south change places
every now and again
as polarities reverse

consequences become new causes
as night turns into a fish
and the day rages

events cascade, language too
has its tipping points

on the verge of

I thought I heard a song
but couldn't catch the air

it came and went
on slights of mind

the pages of the book are flicking
flipping
rushed by wind

I can hear the movement of sad trombones
an unsteady descant

in the minor chords
it all comes to rest

on the edge of the music

any moment now
the melody will come to me

how the years rub

how the years rub
the fabric of a life

each moment
has its moment
before the next
wear and tear

wind passes right through
my old coat
the knees on my trousers shine
my bones give out at the elbow
knuckles turn white

sleep comes only after
I have visited those people
who die in the lonely places

the testimony of the senses

the pendulum sings, a wild metallic sound
follows my meanings
more precisely than artificial intelligence
that can't break the spell
or crack the code

for the line is drawn beyond
the field of computation

there is no accounting for tastes
the same is true of love
the same is true of time
or the origin of mind

the big questions come to grief
on the brilliance of a smile
there's no taking it back

a low cut, perfumed rose, white or red
tells the story
puts the icing on the cake

the mechanical mind can never be free
no matter how many notches it slips

love is a cosmopolitan passion
not the algorithms of the metaverse

or the cold equations of greed
but the nuptials of fire and water

flame floats on its moving surface
a lily pad of crimson
blood and marrow

ah yes, I can't help but think, love
despite the uselessness of thought
that no pretender's blade is
sharp enough
to slice our common heart

where there is, there is not

you can fill up your life with the consolations
of the flesh and the mind
(while others feast on hunger)
and still be inconsolable

you can weep a lifetime of tears
and still feel sad

we can see almost to the other end of time
but our lives are gone in an instant

conflagrations won't put out the fires
ash from the flame
words swept away in the very moment
of their being

fond illusions don't make a world

there is unbeing at the heart
of being

one extra hour

rain, as gentle as glass is smooth
the ground glows
the land breathes

we plant broad beans early
turn the compost, open the earth
focus the blue of morning
feed the chooks and get on with
whatever it may be

the moments hurtle by
mostly unseen
plump sparrows gather for the hen's grain

plum blossoms blush as pink
as in medieval Chinese poems
tūī parties alone
the sparrows scatter
thought shoots in all directions

we'll enjoy our extra hour
we'll spend it together
we won't waste time
we will each be
in the fragrance of the other

we'll stand in the rain, gentle
as glass is smooth

abandoned baby blackbird

even though Daniela kept it at her breast
where warmth flowed
and fed its wide-open mouth
with the choicest meats
out of its nest
the little blackbird died
of strangeness
and grief

hollowed out in the hologram

from the garble and the pixel angels
cavorting on the screen
where cyber words float
in imaginary space

I see a deep fake version of me
cultivated by algorithms
harvested
and sold back to myself
at a price I can never afford

nothing here but the parodies
of unreason

reaching through
the smooth limbed allure
the incantations of the instep
the soldered dreams of blue and green
where the forest grieves

to the day of everyday breathing
and breaking bread and love-making

the rattling in the leaves
the sighing of the leaves
the raking of the leaves
the inhaling of the leaves

the getting goosed among the geese
having a double shot at the shot shop
before the be-bop

as the hour glass spins
I follow myself around
or lose myself
in the jumble of steel and glass
or between the shadows of lost trees
in the grit and the grunt
make believe and jump jazz

to consider, at great length
the screen of night
upon which everything is projected
in a play of coherent light
against the backdrop
of mind

conjurations

voices are fading outside and inside
and in my lady's chamber
where the story's just been told
and the audience is standing up
to shake themselves free
of any conjurations
or sneaky implications
or hidden machinations
lines that bite back

we're all about to hit the street
what did you make of the ending
did it follow from the premise
did love win or lose
was Hamlet really mad
did horses really eat each other
in those distempered times?

angels of vision
barricade the sidewalks with
piano wires strung through their hearts
plucking a dance tune
the last songs
the final spells
distant airs
and distant arias

and there's lots of paper, paper
with words, words
lots of them
words
all in a big long slug-line

yet none strong enough to hold
the peace

so let's hold hands, shall we
until we get to the corner
after which
all bets are off

Mike Johnson, fiction writer and poet, is widely regarded as one of New Zealand's most innovative writers. He lives on Waiheke Island and has taught creative writing at AUT University and the University of Auckland. In 2002 he received The University of Auckland's Literary Fellowship, having been Literary Fellow at Canterbury University in 1987. His first novel, *Lear, the Shakespeare Company Plays Lear at Babylon* was short listed for the New Zealand Book Awards in 1986, his novel *Dumb Show* won the Buckland Memorial Award for Literary Excellence in 1995, and he won the Frances Kean Award for his short story, 'Magic Strings' in 1999. His first book of poetry, *The Palanquin Ropes*, (1983) was co-winner of the John Cowie Reed Memorial Competition. His non-fiction, *Angel of Compassion*, was shortlisted for the Ashton Whyle Award in 2014, and a poem from *Vertical Harp, The selected poems of Li He* (2006) has been anthologised in the *Essential New Zealand Poems: Facing the Empty Page* (Random House, 2015). Mike Johnson is the author of thirty books including eleven books of poetry, three of shorter fiction, one non-fiction, four children's books, and eleven novels.

Also by Mike Johnson

Novels
Afterworld
Stench
Driftdead
Lethal Dose
Zombie in a Spacesuit
Hold My Teeth While I Teach You to Dance
Travesty
Counterpart
Dumbshow
Antibody   Positive
Lear: The Shakespeare Company Plays Lear at Babylon

Shorter Fiction
Confessions of a Cockroach/Headstone
Back in the Day: Tales of NZ's Own Paradise Island
Foreigners

Poetry
The Nine Lives of Willa the Cat, Illustrated by Frances Ryder
Selected Poems
Sketches
The Raising Light Trilogy
Ladder With No Rungs, Illustrated by Leila Lees
Two Lines and a Garden, Illustrated by Leila Lees
To Beatrice: Where We Crossed the Line
Vertical Harp: The Selected Poems of Li He
Treasure Hunt
Standing Wave
From a Woman in Mt Eden Prison & Drawing Lessons
The Palanquin Ropes

Non-Fiction
Angel of Compassion

Children's Books
Flippity Fluppity Flop, Illustrated by Daniela Gast
A House With No Windows, Illustrated by Ingrid Berzins
Kenni and the Roof Slide, Illustrated by Jennifer Rackham
Taniwha. Illustrated by Jennifer Rackham

www.ingramcontent.com/pod-product-compliance
Lightning Source LLC
Chambersburg PA
CBHW031427120626
46545CB00006B/2299